CorporateSnippets
empowering hearts

Because Young Adults Have Hearts 2!

Corporate America doesn't care! Yes, it is a young America, but most young people don't even know how business was conducted thirty years ago.

Now, imagine a special place everyone knows as Mom & Pops shop. On the front porch, there are a few rocking chairs, maybe a table with a large pitcher of ice-cold lemonade enticing people in the community to sit, chit chat and refresh themselves.

The atmosphere inside is pleasant as well, maybe more so as it is always warm, cheerful, and inviting. There may not be a lot of offerings, but always on the menu are kind words, a helpful attitude to everyone, and a genuine appreciation for the opportunity to serve.

The person behind the counter is usually the owner, but whoever the person is, they welcome you with a smile, often calling you by your name, as they excitedly try to help you.

Their sincere manner and serving attitude make you feel wanted and appreciated. There is always the thank-you and please come again. These sincere words add to the pleasure of spending both your time and your hard-earned money.

Leaving with your purchase, or just having enjoyed the friendly setting, you feel good as you anticipate your next visit.

The past is the past, however, we can better our best from her lessons.

So, allow the above walk down memory lane to remind some of us and, maybe introduce to others the simplicity, as well as the importance of care for others in any setting.

The Company Of ... because we all care, we all need a hand-up at times, and we all influence others by design or default, yes, we all lead others in some manner.

***

Introducing

Corporate <u>SNIPPETS</u> - The Company Of ...

Blends the spirit of care from Mom & Pop Shops of old with the novelties of *today* to empower hearts, one's own, and the hearts of others.

***

Growing older is mandatory; growing wise is a choice! Do not allow age to define nor determine your leadership ability and capabilities.

Young Adults - stand tall. Embrace your uniqueness by allowing the inspirations of your heart to create the rhythms of your life.

Choose to **own** your power because purposeful care for other people is creating your legacy.

Corporate SNIPPETS – The Company Of ...

Because Young Adults Have **HEARTS** 2!

***

People Talk about

Corporate SNIPPETS –
The Company Of ...

This book is an inspiring collection of prose, encouragement, and guidance for those interested in developing the leader within. The true nature of leadership is helping people and sometimes that means sacrificing your desires for the good of others.

Women have hearts leadership includes assessments and questions to help you discover and accept your strengths. Helping people is what leadership is all about! Hope this helps!

V. Lyles, Office Manager

Yes, this does help and as a Woman, in the business arena, your great words are surely from first-hand knowledge. Thanks for your time and effort reviewing this book.

***

This is great! Thank you for sharing! I think this will resonate with a lot of people in my generation, "Gen Z"; many of them are entrepreneurial, want to pursue business, are spiritually inclined, and want to pursue self-improvement.

J. Johnson, Student

As a young person about to graduate college and start on your entrepreneurial desires, I appreciate your input and sincerely hope this book will help other young adults to love hearts, their own and others.

***

As a consumer aka customer and worker in Corporate America, I like the major message I got from this publication and that was encouraging business professionals to care for people. This care is aimed at the ones behind the counter and those stepping up to the courter, as I've done both. And, especially today in a pandemic, all I hear is people talk about the poorness of customer service or that it does not seem to exist today.

I also like that this book will help generations behind my own to know that we can create *thriving businesses and STILL treat people good.*

I also like that many young people may not know about Mom-and-Pop stores, and this publication may open their eyes and help them instill this philosophy in their business personality.

R. Mai, Entrepreneur

You hit on points I sincerely hope are covered here, so thanks for taking time to review this publication. I wish you continued success with your business endeavors.

***

I like your book and can tell you put a lot of thought and effort into it. I believe people will get a lot from it, especially people who manage others. I can tell you put your heart and soul into creating it. My only suggestion is that you do not have the many genres together in one book.

L. Ealey – Claims Administrator

Thanks, first all for your honest assessment. We followed your advice, and this project has grown into the series:

Corporate SNIPPETS –
The Company Of ...

***

A heart-felt message to You, Young heart:

Caring, inspiring, and purposeful efforts are not about age...

A leadership mindset starts from within and grows. Young people take pride in your uniqueness. Do not feel you must be one in the crowd.

Yes, indifference from others hurt. It pinches the heart, but it does not have to crush your spirit. Recognize you do not have to fit in and go along to get along.

With a Leader's attitude, charge forward creating your path. Do not try and be like everyone else.

Please allow the message of this book help you love on that best part of you, your heart, growing, flowing, and spreading to touch others.

***

Let's brainstorm...

1. What are your hobbies?

2. What do you like to read or talk about?

3. What are your natural talents?

4. What TV shows do you enjoy, and why?

5. What information or help do others seek from you often?

6. What is your passion - something you love to do, something you cannot imagine yourself NOT doing?

7. What can you share by way of showing, telling, or teaching?

8. Where is there a void in the market today? Can you provide a service or product to fill this void?

9. What nags at you? What is tedious; and do you have a way to make it better?

Young heart – remember, a future is too close and too important to chance – especially Yours!

Once you discover a true love, something you are good at, something you are passionate about, something your gut tells you to *go for,* it is time to move forward.

When we follow our heart's passion and do what we love, success will follow, because we are shaped by what we love.

Now, realize success looks different for everyone, so, determine what success looks and feels like for you.

Be open to exploring. Try new possibilities because there is something rejuvenating about new, different, and/or improved.

A few more thoughts:

- Do you possess a pioneer spirit?
- Do you view yourself a visionary?
- Do you have faith in your abilities?
- Are you committed to your success?
- Do you have self-motivation?
- And, as important as the above - do you believe in helping others succeed?

Don't follow the path - create your own. Choose to brand your life an adventure, not a happenstance.

***

I Believe!

There is something special about someone who believes they have what it takes to succeed? Determined, they forge ahead in a state of I Believe!

What is there without belief? What will get you to the mountaintop? How is there some way, when before there was none?

Does it all come back to I Believe? The principle is easy to understand, and so, pleasing when achieved - being many parts of

I Believe.

I Believe I Am Value.

I Believe I Can to all possibilities

I Believe I deserve Life's Glory.

I Believe in ME!

***

Because Young Adults Have Hearts 2!

Table of Contents:

Introduction ...

<u>Expressions</u> ...

Your Gift

At birth, you inherited the best gift you have or ever will receive. Now, as the Guardian of this gift, and as with most gifts, you control how you love and honor, protect, cherish, and grow it.

Now, unlike most gifts, re-gifting is essential, so...

Care for it, and ***watch*** it bloom.

Replenish it; it ***renews*** again and again.

Expand it; it ***reaches*** inspiring someone in a special way.

Value it; it **strengthens** others.

Give it; it ***comes back***, bigger, better, and stronger.

Leave it; it ***binds*** holding tight.

Live it; and ***reap*** its mighty influences.

Love it; it ***gives*** keeping love in motion.

This perfect gift - <u>Your</u> Heart

Because you own the powers of your heart, remember your heart must learn, laugh, love, and grow to thrive, to give, and, to live.
Yep, it is this simple.

***

A Leader's Heart

I possess the heart of a Leader –
Not because of riches or fame
But for the simple pleasure of doing for another
what I can.
Helping someone is not something new
It's something we all can do.
It's helping by design - it's there deep inside…
Continuing to shine – when it's sharing time.
There's great value to accrue, because
What flows from the heart ALWAYS circles
back to you.
It's a boomerang effect –
So, I'll make a heart smile, and go that extra
mile. I make a difference in people's lives.

I Am A Leader!

***

My Heart Declaration!

I claim ownership of My Heart.

I Know My Heart is always hungry and needs daily loving care, and will take in what it is fed.

I realize what I feed My Heart creates the liveliness, the motivation, and the specialness in my life.

So, I will do more than merely feed My Heart, I choose to <u>feast</u> from the good fruit life offers.

And I pledge to cherish *"The Gift"* of My Heart by sharing it with others.

My Heart Declaration!

Name _____

Date _____

***

You and I,

You and I own qualities that affect others.

You and I possess the strengths to help someone.

You and I have love in our hearts to share.

You and I,

The Company Of ...

Young Adult Leaders!

Because leading from the heart is not an age thing; it is a love for people thing!

***

To BE or to become...

Choose to BE a better version of you every day!   Do not fall into the trap of fixing yourself.

Do not allow defined flaws of others to shape your growth path.

BE you through knowledge, and nurturance of your strengths.

Human influences make growth a constant; so, dust off, re-commit and honor the invisible contract you made at birth to love, and appreciate YOU for a lifetime.

Do not try to become.

BE YOU.

***

I Am

I am in a good place.

All is well with my world.

My soul is full of joy.

My mind is unconstrained.

I am heartened by family and friends.

My heart is open.

There is a light in ME.

I will pass it on and share it with others.

These, the strengths of I Am!

***

Mirror Truths

Check your mirror before peering at others to judge them, or when you don't understand someone.

Does your mirror reveal a casualness in your care of others?

Are there many tiny cracks of entitlement reflected in your mirror? OR does it reveal a heart full of gratefulness?

Check your mirror – are you the best friend you can be for someone?

Does your mirror show you standing still or moving forward?

Now, look deep – does your mirror give a clear view of you? Do you see someone growing into all he or she can be?

Now - the most important mirror truth - whose face smiles back full of love flowing to others!

***

Empowering Hearts

Hearts-fed *to* **hearts-led** is actively feeding one's heart so well it blossoms, blooms, and spreads. It is caring and valuing the growth of self and others because the *better* you take care of your heart, the *more* you can share it with others.

Caring for the hearts of others requires conscious effort. It is the intent of this publication that these stirrings of *passion*, *purpose*, and *practices* open the hearts of young adults to share love always.

*Now, a caveat as we realize all people may not have the same intentions towards others as is the focus of this publication.

The Company Of ...
Together, let us learn, laugh, love, and grow giving of our Heart.

***

Not a random read...

Why this publication?
We desire this publication to help all of us recognize we all need to feel validated and appreciated, regardless of our age.

We all want to know we are vital part of our community and are appreciated.

What should you do with this publication?
Use it to strengthen yourself and to become more conscious of your mindset and actions when dealing with people. Use it to remind yourself - when people are involved – hearts are involved, and hearts *always* matter.

What will you get from this publication?
This publication will serve you best with daily use. The *passion*, *purpose*, and *practices* in leadership success will keep your heart involved and focused on all your interactions with people.

Allow these simple messages of love and care grow your heart and spread to others because amazing things seldom happen by chance.

***

The Company Of ...
<u>Expressions</u>

Heart – a blessed gift housing our specialness.

Corporate – Business – Community – settings that involve people relating among themselves and others.

Corporate <u>SNIPPETS</u> – blends the spirit of love and care from the old, with patterns of today creating a *people-centered*, *heart-focused* setting where care and attention are tools of growth for all.

> **<u>SNIPPETS</u>** – eight action-driven, life-changing collective attitudes.

> **Snippitude** – The synergies of the 8 <u>SNIPPETS</u> inspiring a proactive approach to living grateful, positive, and fruitful lives.

SnippTips – mini entrepreneurial prompts meshed with character/lifestyle tips to activate care in any people-engaged setting.

Snippetpreneur – People who nourish and nurture the hearts of people purposefully.

Raise Them Up! – The theme song for Sunshine4Hearts Brands.

B.Y.O.B. - **Bring Your Own Best** - wired up aiming for excellence in all you do.

Poraso – bits of poetry, rap, and song together keeping hearts strong.

The Company Of... – tag implies the connecting of like-minded people learning, laughing, loving, and growing together.

Leader – people who aspire to encourage, enlighten, and empower others through acts of teaching *to* learn, sharing *to* grow, and connecting *to* empower.

Hearts-fed *to* Hearts-led – fulling one's hearts with so much of Life's good (leaving little room for her bad) that it spills over to others.

Ways of Hearts-fed *to* hearts-led

- Start with a mindset of helping
- Appreciate people
- Make sure what you bring to the table is the best it can be
- Teach others by your actions
- **<u>A Biggie</u>** - Love what you do – it shows

Learn, Laugh, Love – The heart of something is the learning, laughing, and loving *invested* in it; and the learning, laughing, and loving *shaped* by it.

These Expressions – sprinkled throughout to warm, excite, entertain, and empower your young heart.

***

Section 1

Passion Inspires...

Look *up* for Good Things.

Look *within* for Love, it's your birthright.

Look *forward* to BE a better you.

Look *around* to Serve others.

Look *after* to Bring others along.

Look *in* your Heart for love.

There lies the passion!

Feed your heart good. Feed it often and share the feed to Be Blessed with Love always.

***

Passion Motivators...

We search for passion!

The inspiration for our passion often simmers, it is just within reach. It's there – until – something awakens it and sets it on fire.

Passion is what we do out of love, it's the stimulant that motivates the heart activating greatness. Sharing what you love grows the joy in your heart.

Now, let's focus on the word joy - Is joy and happiness the same? Happiness appears to be conditional; something that is movable, something we can create and *experience,* I'm happy because…

Now, joy is a constant *residing* deep within, a stable serenity, a sense of gladness not activated by external stimuli.

So many ways to describe joy; beauty, balance, harmony, an inner peacefulness affecting all you do.

Work hard to cherish this sweet feeling and allow the joy in your soul to warm your heart always.

***

Feed Your Heart Good

50 Ways:

1. Meditate
2. Read an inspiring book
3. Write a poem to someone special (yourself, maybe)
4. Delight in another's success
5. Comfort a friend
6. Walk your dog
7. Show someone simple kindness
8. Cherish help from others
9. Inhale the fresh aroma of a rainbow
10. Be a blessing to someone in need.
11. Improve a skill
12. Share something special with a friend
13. Go for a walk
14. Make a funny face
15. Do what warms your heart every day
16. Eat an apple
17. Borrow a quality you admire
18. Spread positive and uplifting news
19. Visit the park
20. Expect great things

21. Sit and reflect
22. Practice gratitude
23. Help a friend – don't wait to be asked
24. Participate in a sports activity
25. Wear that outfit that makes you shine
26. Smile for absolutely no reason
27. Forgive a hurt (for you, not someone else)
28. Give thanks
29. Choose to embrace life's lessons
30. Make a new friend
31. View yourself happy
32. Grow self by helping someone every day
33. Appreciate another's point of view
34. Discover something new about you
35. Influence on purpose
36. Pick a flower for someone special
37. Choose to look at whatever your do in a different way
38. Play with a friend
39. Talk lovingly to yourself
40. Believe you are victorious
41. Put your feet up
42. Nurture what is special about you
43. Daydream and see what you want to be
44. Do something extra nice for someone

45. Take a bubble bath
46. Drink lots of water
47. Look for ways to help your friends
48. Sing a song (even off-key)
49. Be sure to learn and laugh every day
50. Keep love in front of ALL you do.

50 Ways, and always growing…

***

Bring Your Own Best
B.Y.O.B.

Bring Your Own Best in all you do.

Let it shine, spread, and help others too.

Not just average or good enough will do.

Choose to spotlight the best of you.

Bring Your Own Best is being true to you.

Not a beginning, it's there – always a part of

you.

Bring Your Own Best is never taboo.

To step to the task.

Bringing Your Own Best - Whatsoever You

Do!

**Bettering one's best is a lifetime
commitment. Maintain an attitude to
generate excellence in all you do.**

***

Go Out and Reach for it...

Passion armed with purpose activates practices. These stirrings create the platform to go out and reach for one's goals.

The Company Of ... assumes, because of the gift of our heart, we have inborn care for others. Because you own the power of your influence, be sure it is positive, purposeful, and empowering.

Appreciate young heart, your leadership skills are born from great followers, as the two exchange as needed. Today, you lead, tomorrow, you follow

The term go out and reach for it, signifies consistent purposeful activity, as seldom does a one-time attempt fulfill goals.

Do not stand still. Get up with a purpose. Reach for it. Perform well. Be proud.

Know when it's time for stillness, or when the situation calls for you to go out and reach for it.

***

Section 2

Purposeful Motives…

So much about the word, purpose, as it motivates us to help others. This motivation is a great way to define and establish parameters for goals, your own, and those you help.

- **Instinct** – Is instinct the same as intuition? Is it a hunch for what may work and what will not work in your leaders' bag of skills?

- **Audacity** – what is your take on this word? Boldness is a characteristic, so sometimes, we must conquer our fear and be bold and sensational. Yes, it takes guts to step out and help someone.

- **Time** – what do we do with our time? All of us have the same amount of time, and when used sensibly time becomes one of life's most valuable resources. Never forget that although time is free, it is priceless.

- **Energy** – Without it - guess what, life can be very dull. The cool thing about energy is how it can turn into synergy when we share to create something special with others.

- **Drive** – ok, is the purpose and drive the same? Does your purpose create the drive? Does drive always follow purpose? What is one without the other?

- **Good Habits** – are behaviors developing over a lifetime and are essential in accomplishing one's goals.

A Leader's focus creates the mindset for helping people. Allow yours to be guided by your desire to help others.

Ok, can we simply say – these six purposeful motives are effective in caring for hearts, one's own, and the hearts of others?

***

Hungry Hearts Feed...

Early on, deep within hungry hearts start to
feed.
Feed your heart frustration – it delivers hurt.
Feed it vengeful acts – it produces chaotic
lives.
Feed it ungrateful thoughts – it weeps.
Feed it heartbreak – it explodes in anger.
Feed it unspeakable sadness – it shows up as
crushing pain.

Why not...

Feed your heart joy for a purposeful walk and

zest to your talk.

Feed it love that blossom spilling over to

others.

Feed it generosity for goodness without

bounds.

Feed it compassion to surround others with

care.

Because Young Adults Have Hearts 2!

Feed it hope, to open wide the mighty doors of

the universe.

Feed it awe for life's grand promises.

Hungry hearts will feed because that is what they do. Choose to love you best by keeping the quest to feed your heart the best of things blessed.

***

Dedication

My writing was inspired by a great motivational writer, and speaker, Dr. Virgie Binford, who gave me eight empowering titles.

I created the essence of these titles into eight life-enriching principles, **The 8 <u>SNIPPETS</u>**.

I remember our many breakfasts at Aunt Sarah's Pancake House in Richmond VA. Of course, food was not on my mind, learning from this beautiful and loving soul was my food choice.

So, another testimony for the small woman with the big booming voice and the biggest, brightest smile I have ever seen.

Rest in peace Virgie. Thanks for helping me claim my passion, you are in my heart forever.

***

<u>Life</u> <u>Enrichment</u> <u>Cycles</u>

The 8 **<u>SNIPPETS</u>**©

Known as scrap, fragments, odds and ends
And other strangeness of one's mind.
Because everything grows over time
Now The 8 <u>SNIPPETS</u> of 2021 and Beyond
Are Feel-good motivators that have spawned
To purposeful acts of sharing
Helping someone who may have gone astray
Or those needing a touch, just to improve their
day.
Here you have them
Eight tools to elevate and motivate
Know them here as helpmates

Eights <u>SNIPPETS</u> to measure
Eight <u>SNIPPETS</u> to treasure
Growth from helping others
Now, that's a real pleasure.

The 8 <u>SNIPPETS</u> grew out of nothing becoming...

- **dreams** – *promoting curiosity* for life's endless possibilities

- **concepts & values** – guides for *bettering one's best* self

- **desire** to *create and share something spectacular*

- **action** triggers to *make things happen*

***

Eight life-enrichment cycles...

Bricks and mortar are the make-up of a cold, impersonal, and motionless structure.

Now, a community is made of people - people who love, hurt, become wounded, celebrate happiness, people with hearts.

It is the people within molding care and hospitality that creates the personality of the community. These same people represent and promote the brand as well as nurture customers.

*Allow the **SNIPPETS** life enrichment cycles nurture your soul by loving and helping you share your heart.*

***

The 32 Days & Ways of SNIPPETS (T32DWS)

T32DWS have the wherewithal to create dreams with its brainstorming practices.

T32DWS helps you create tactics to get where you want to go because actions of today creates tomorrow's success.

Here we align and connect - **The 8 SNIPPETS & T32DWS (a potent combination)** to energize young hearts to *dream big*, to *plan purposefully*; and to *step boldly* to the future they imagine.

First, The 8 SNIPPETS...

***

Stir the soul with ideas...

This <u>SNIPPET</u> grows *personal commitment* to keep your core, your heart stimulated, and primed for growing and sharing.

(What is your major commitment to yourself?)

T32DWS #1 - It is not that serious...

Today, I will view my life as an exciting adventure of learning, laughing, loving, and growing

T32DWS #2 - Treasure the power of hope...

Today, I will create magic in my life…

T32DWS #3 - Not failure; an education...

Today, I will forget the mistakes of the past, but remember their lessons…

<u>N</u>egotiate with an attitude of gratitude...

This <u>SNIPPET</u> focuses on the *power of a heart filled with respect and thankfulness.*

(At this time in my life, I am most thankful for...?)

<u>T32DWS #4 - Thankfulness always...</u>

Today, I will appreciate all my blessings.

<u>T32DWS #5 - Let go of the ego; it is man-made...</u>

Today, I will let go of my need to be right, it is not as much right or wrong, but the lesson learned...

<u>T32DWS #6 - Stimulation creates growth...</u>

Today, I will try something different...

<u>T32DWS #7 - Strength in flexibility...</u>

Today, I will not put a limit on my dreams, I'll see where they take me instead...

Incorporate strength builders for success...

This SNIPPET teaches us to *embrace challenges as opportunities to better our best every day.*

**(Today, my most pressing challenge is...*?)*

T32DWS #8 - Believe in the force of self...

Today, I will use my strong points to accomplish goals.

T32DWS #9 - Truth is key...

Today, I will do what I know is right…

T32DWS #10 - It is good being me...

Today, I will treat myself with compassion…

T32DWS #11 - Responsibility is a choice ...

Today, I will be accountable to myself…

T32DWS #12 - Excitement empowers...

Today, I will embrace my enthusiasm and use it as a tool for growth…

Notes

Pair similarities for positive reinforcement...

This <u>SNIPPET</u> suggests *looking beyond surface differences* as avenues for growth.

(What lessons can I borrow from others for reaching my goals?)

T32DWS #13 - Exploring creates a desire for action...

Today, I will keep moving; standing still is not an option…

T32DWS #14 – My Thoughts rule...

Today, I will stand strong and proud in my beliefs…

T32DWS #15 - Appreciate life is not stagnant...

Today, I will look at the choices showing up in my life as opportunities…

T32DWS #16 - Creative thoughts shape spirited lives...

Today, I will allow only positive, motivating, and uplifting beliefs to take hold.

Notes

Pave roads of progress for safe travel...

This SNIPPET stresses the importance of *aligning hearts with a purposeful plan of action* for achieving goals.

(Now, are my goals constant, action-driven, and measurable?)

T32DWS #17 - If one way does not work, try another...

Today, I will maintain a watchful eye on the prize…

T32DWS #18 - Rest, mend and grow...

Today, I will relax in the gap between where I am and where I am going…

T32DWS #19 - Learn from watching...

Today, I will stay in the moment with purposeful attention…

T32DWS #20 - Training betters the best...

Today, I will exercise my body as well as my mind…

<u>Notes</u>

Expect the best in creative projects...

This <u>SNIPPET</u> harnesses *the power of belief.*

(Some of my strongest beliefs about life, love, and business are …?)

<u>T32**DWS** #21 - **Faith**</u>...

Today, I will anticipate success…

<u>T32**DWS** #22 - **Awareness opens doors**</u>...

Today, I will explore what I need to know to grow…

<u>T32**DWS** #23 - **Love grows when it flows**</u>...

Today, I will cherish the joy in my soul…

<u>T32**DWS** #24 - **Be a part to have a part**</u>...

Today, I will nurture my friends…

Think and design, lead and teach...

This <u>SNIPPET</u> highlights the *(seemingly)* *magical power of our thoughts* to *create* real-life events in our lives.

(How do I create the needed quiet moments of my life to allow my thoughts to surface?)

T32DWS #25 - People keep the world growing...

Today, I will build bridges with others appreciating the powers of synergy...

T32DWS #26 - Listen well; learn wisely...

Today, I will sharpen my listening and comprehension skills...

T32DWS #27 - The influence of (my) words...

Today, I will erase the words could, should, and would from my vocabulary...

T32DWS #28 - Challenges, choices, and change are the growth patterns of life...

Today, I will step through my fears…

Notes

<u>S</u>hare and support gems of wisdom by authority...

This <u>SNIPPET</u> carries *elements of value for others while providing unlimited growth opportunities for self.*

(Some of the best of me I share with others are...?)

<u>T32DWS #29 - Lend a hand wherever you can...</u>

Today, I will care enough to share...

<u>T32DWS #30 - Keep knowledge in motion...</u>

Today, I will find satisfaction in sharing my accomplishments...

<u>T32DWS #31 - All is well in my world...</u>

Today, I will laugh with family, friends, and people I care about...

T32DWS #32 - <u>**Caring gestures create huge results**</u>...

<u>Today, I will strive for excellence, not perfection…</u>

The **<u>SNIPPETS</u>** greatest intent is the ability to mushroom itself into many affirming ways.

They complement **The 32 Days & Ways of SNIPPETS** meshed with the power in **Today, I Will.**

So, what is the significance of the thirty-two days?

You and I, The Company Of … we can use the power of our *thoughts* to have use of an additional day when needed, hence - the thirty-two days of - <u>Today, I Will</u>.

***

Section 3

Practices ...

PRACTICES

Positive **R**evitalizing **A**ctivating **C**hoices
That **I**nspire **C**reative **E**mpowered **S**elves

1. Belief

2. Mindfulness

3. Thanks

4. Integrity

5. Joy

6. Victory

7. Ministry

8. Ideas

9. Learning

10. Love

The PRACTICES ...

- *promotes* a caring mindset ... their own for the benefit of being there for others.

- *stimulate* growth for self ... to pass on to others.

- *enhance* compassion ... knowing we all need help from others at some time.

- *magnify* mindfulness for others.

- *foster* positive and purposeful influence.

At times, we are callous to others by what we do, and what we say. Because this is usually un-intentional, please allow the *practices* to help keep you engaged with others in a caring and thoughtful manner.

Corporate <u>SNIPPETS</u>

Empowering Hearts!

***

The Practice of Extreme Care

First, let us break this down – practicing extreme care is an active commitment to knowing, loving, appreciating, and growing self.

Know self to appreciate and love self. Loving you better allows you to love others more. We have all experienced "there is already too much emphasis on loving self", and "loving self too much is arrogant and causes people to care only about themselves".

Now, a healthy fixation on self is *first*, believing in who you are and what you are about. *Second*, loving yourself is just that – taking good care of yourself. Not just the outer self, but the inner part where hearts live.

And *third,* and most important – to care and grow self makes it easy to care for and help others grow.

Caring for others is a love for people thing!

The **passion**, **purpose**, and **practices** in this publication is aimed at keeping you in the front and center of your own life, nurturing the love for self to spread and touch others.

***

Corporate <u>SNIPPETS</u>...Dear Leader:

Twenty-two heart-inspired letters to people (young or old) who care about people. No, it is not a million-dollar design, as there are no bells and whistles or floating icons, nor a lot of fluff to entice, but do not add long-lasting value.

However, this **passion**, **purpose**, **and practice** in success leadership has a million-dollar intent, the *care for the hearts of all people.*

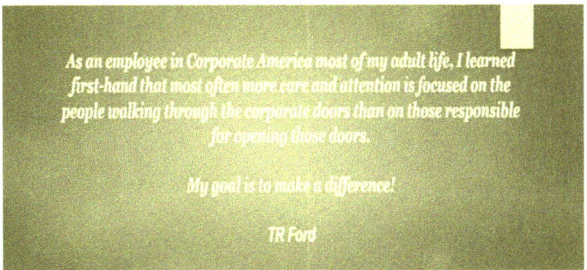

When people are involved, hearts are involved, and yes - hearts always matter, so <u>R</u>aise <u>T</u>hem <u>U</u>p, the hearts of people!

***

Because Young Adults Have Hearts 2!

All people-oriented communities house two centers.

- First, the <u>excitement</u> and <u>passion</u> center - composed of people, relationships, creativity (company's vision, innovation, etc.).

- <u>Technology, financial systems</u>, and <u>marketing</u> compose the second center.

Each Center is crucial, as one will not work without the other. Each *serves* as the heart of a community, and each *service* the hearts in any community.

The **"WHY"** ... Because hearts are in the mix, head, and heart-conscious efforts must be involved. Choosing to find ways to grow yourself helps to grow any community you are a part of.

To summarize - search for ways to help grow any endeavor you are a part of.

***

<u>The Great Reveal!</u>

You, and I
We expect to be valued.
We desire love.
We care for those we love.
We want what we believe we deserve.
We want to grow and better our best selves.
You, and I – <u>We</u> are the WHO,
because we all need care and help from others.

You, and I –
The Company of ...

***

Corporate Snippets
empowering hearts

Highlights HOW
Corporate
SNIPPETS...
Dear Leader:

   a. Each Letter **starts** with a question requiring thought and reflection.

b. Each Letter **contains** relevant heart-warming content with a **Ponder this...** snippet.

c. Each Letter **ends** with a thoughtful, engaging, and empowering PostScript.

The "**HOW**", as growth comes from all aspects of living grateful and thankful lives.

Think about this – is it possible to grow when feelings of entitlement dominate your spirit?

Being grateful for what you already have may be the door opener to more.

***

Your Calling

Dear Leader:

What is your calling?

It's a beautiful fall morning as we listen to Pastor explore all the wonders of helping others. He spoke about the missionary work of the Church. Pastor then explained that a Missionary cannot be a success all by themselves. Missionary work is about educating, supporting, sharing, and caring with and for others.

He said missionary work is not just a need in foreign lands but must start first in our backyard. Missionary work is not just in the guise of Church people, but Missionaries walk in my shoes as well as yours.

Ponder this... Is a Missionary simply an influencer, simply someone who cares for another?

- So, do you perform a missionary's work in your school, or social activities?

- Do you connect with or join in with people when they are trying to make a difference?

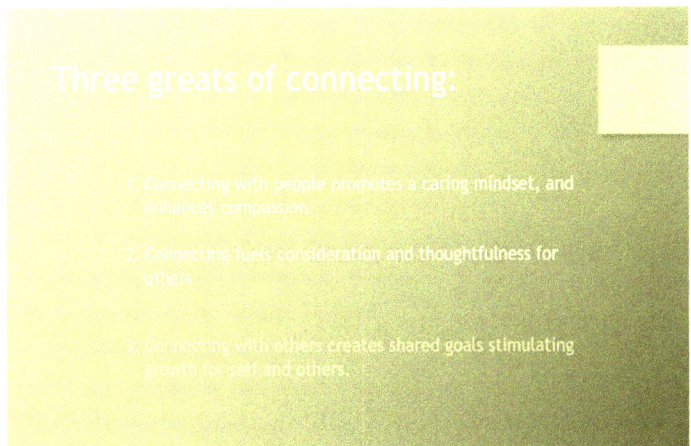

A Calling, A Ministry, A Leader - whatever we choose to call purposeful connectedness and care for another - it is good to reach out because no one makes it alone.

P. S. Young heart - whatever the title, be sure to sprinkle pieces of your heart wherever you are...

***

The Quest for Respect

Corporate Snippets
empowering hearts

January 1, 2XXX

Dear Leader:

Why the quest for respect?

Respect me because like you, I hurt, and I've been wounded.

Respect me, it's not hard, and it's the right thing to do.

Respect me although I do not look, talk, or live like you.

Respect me to better you, as respect is earned.

Respect me as a valued person, one loyal, evolving, and growing.

Respect my beauty, my strength, and my motivation.

Respect me for my desire to grow my family strong, healthy, and wise.

Respect my belief in the good of people.

Respect me for honoring my Mother and Father and for treating all people decently.

Because Young Adults Have Hearts 2!

Ponder this... Is **respect** a huge demand, or is it the small gestures of care, and the slices of kindness we share?

The effects of respect can disarm foes, mend broken fences, and help people feel appreciated and cared for.

P.S. What would our world look like if the practice of respect is at the front of all people-involved endeavors.

***

Yes, People First – Always!

January 1, 2XXX

Dear Leader:

How do you see your parents, coaches, friends, teachers, and schoolmates?

Do you see them as *people with needs, wants, dreams, and aspirations?*

Do you see them as *people who are part of a family that fellowship, learn, laugh, and love with each other?*

Do you see them as *people with likes and dislikes?*

Do you see them as *people who want to feel special, who want to feel appreciated?*

Think about how you choose to SEE those you interact with. The way you see someone is how you will treat and or respond to them.

When those around you or in your circle feel respect and care from you, they will treat you and others special.

Ponder this... How does your caring mindset help you mature?

The answer is simply - *care for people and lend a hand – yours – wherever and whenever you can.*

With people, it is all about the heart – keeping it warm, vital and in motion helping others.

P.S. Remember, science fiction movies teach us that robots are <u>programmed</u> for top performance. In real life - people are <u>loved</u> to perform their best.

***

Power in the intangibles...

January 1, 20XX

Dear Leader:

What are the intangibles in your life?

Is it is composed of the many things of life we cannot see or touch?

Can we call these *things* goodwill? So, what is goodwill? Is it simple acts of kindness and thoughtfulness of another? What makes goodwill so valuable for all people?

Ponder this... Is there a better time than now, for all of us to show simple kindness to others? Let's remember the mom-and-pop shops of old where the intangibles such as genuine care, hospitality, and a helpful demeanor were always at the top of the menu.

Young heart – strive to keep *these things*, the goodwill alive - growing, stirring, and spreading!

P.S. Embrace the power of *these things*, the invisible, always there and a part of our lives in all ways.

***

The Question!

January 1, 20XX

Dear Leader:

What's In It For Me?

Yes, yes, we know everyone tunes into the popular station, What's In It For Me (WIIFM).

This question, what's in it for me is not always appropriate. Do for others because being focused only on "What's In It For Me" is not a sincere way to help others.

Ponder this... Allow the answer to, What's In It for Me become – I am happy and pleased when my efforts help another person succeed.

P.S. Ask yourself often, What's In It For Others to be sure the answer is one of helping someone.

***

Because Young Adults Have **Hearts** 2!

The Golden Rule!

January 1, 20XX

Dear Leader:

What is the important message of the "Golden Rule" and how does it apply to my life?

How do you treat people?

- Do you treat your classmates with care and consideration?

- If someone is being bullied, do you step in to help them?

- Do you show all people, not just your elders respect, honor and good manners?

Now, what if...

You were to treat everyone you touch with the way you want to be treated?

Because Young Adults Have Hearts 2!

Now, is this the true message of The Golden Rule.

Now, this question deserves careful thought because the way you treat people is most likely how they will treat you.

Ponder this... Most often, the way we treat other people is the way we are treated. So, yes, the specialness of the "Golden Rule" applies to every part of living gracious, and loving lives.

P. S. The message of the "Golden Rule" will stand the test of time!

***

What defines a great Leader?

January 1, 20XX

Dear Leader:

Are remarkable Leaders only in history books?

OK, know this; responsive and caring Leaders walk in your shoes as well as mine.

Great leadership is not a business ideal. Empowering leadership starts in the mind as *a way of being* and then spreads to *a way of doing,* both stemming from genuine care for people.

The most promising trait of a good leader is their belief in the good of people. They use their passion, resourcefulness, and expertise to help others.

Yes, young heart – learning will teach you leadership disciplines, but true leadership stems from the heart.

Because Young Adults Have Hearts 2!

Leaders grow themselves so their gifts and abilities are on point, able to help others.

Ponder this... Who you are is what you do. Caring leadership is not a one-time, some-time special event, but a conscious everyday effort!

P. S. Leadership is not something you wear or put on. Leadership is something deep within you that yearns to help others move forward.

***

The Synergy of Leadership!

January 1, 20XX

Dear Leader:

What are three things needed for success?

1. *Realize growth never ends.* These Leaders seek ways to keep themselves motivated, informed, and able.

2. *Lives one's passion,* These Leaders believe in what they are doing and committed to do the best they can.

3. *Sharers.* These Leaders grow their talents by sharing as they realize sharing helps them to better their best selves.

Ponder this... There is a skill to genuine leadership composed of awareness, care, and heart-felt influences.

P. S. So, is synergy simply stirring people hearts and efforts toward a common goal?

***

The Grit of a Leader...

January 1, 20XX

Dear Leader:

Do you have a Leader's Grit?

Is your attitude ripe to - Teach to learn - Share to grow - Connect to empower!

Ponder this... When we view ourselves as a teacher, we learn. When we become avid contributors to others, we grow and when we connect, we empower. Cultivating the growth of others is a byproduct and a sure path to growth for ourselves.

Ponder this... An attitude of care and understanding creates opportunities to help others.

P. S. We were taught as children to *play* together. We now know, it was not simply

children playing, but lessons in growing ourselves while helping to ensure the growth of others.

***

Leadership Traits, Tools, and Strategies:

January 1, 20XX

Dear Leader:

What is your best gift to share?

Your gifts are the qualities, characteristics, individual traits, and attributes you possess.

We all possess Leadership gifts that can help someone, and the most important thing about a gift is sharing it.

Ponder this... Every Leader brings his or her own unique talents of special influences, challenges, and personal truths to the table.

P.S. What are some traits you admire most in others? Have you taken the time to consider

if these traits are, as well, a part of your repertoire?

***

The Optimist Creed!

January 1, 20XX

Dear Leader:

Optimistic – hopeful, confident, positive, cheerful, sanguine, bright, buoyant, full of hope

Ponder this... Is the glass half-full or half-empty?

<u>The Optimist Creed!</u>
Promise yourself to be so strong that nothing can disturb your peace of mind.

Christian D. Larson

P. S. The Optimist Creed! - so appropriate for inspiring and motivating leaders because

some of us look for the good to pull from a situation, and then some of us look for the bad.

Now, here is the key, each of us will get exactly what we look for.

***

Raise Them Up!

January 1, 20XX

Dear Leader:

Do people make the world go around?

- People want to feel special, appreciated, and treated with respect.

Care for people by creating ways to help them...

Intentionally raise your spirit and consciousness toward others.

Help to raise their appreciation and pride in themselves and their expectations for growth.

Yes, you have the power to Raise Them Up – hearts of mankind.

Raise Them Up!

Raise Them Up Spiritually, Purposely, Publicly

Each one for The Other...

Raise Them Up Creatively, Heartily,

Intellectually - Your Hearts and Mine.

Raise Them Up Socially, So - Happily, Opening

Doors - Expecting More.

Raise Them Up Actively, Vigorously, Yes, It's

Time for Hearts to Shine

Hearts of Mankind.

Raise Them Up My Brother and Me, SO

Lovingly, Their Hearts

Yours and Mine

Raise Them Up...

P.S. As a growing leader - Be Better - Be Different - Do More to Raise Them _U_p!

***

Because Young Adults Have Hearts 2!

88 SnippTips

Creating high levels of concern for people keeping hearts fed well Today, and Tomorrow.

Young Leaders - embrace these SnippTips to grow into and strengthen your leadership capability. Allow them to help you step with boldness; confident you have the heart and mind to care, and lead, and to do it well.

SnippTip #1
It is all about your **attitude** - which is a personal choice you make.

Thought to ponder – What major attitude about yourself do you need to improve; one that will also warm your heart?

SnippTip #2

Caring gestures spread, invigorating all in its path, so make a conscious effort to help people be their best selves.

Thought to ponder – What simple, yet thoughtful acts of care set you apart from other people?

Connect to create.

Thought to ponder – Get rid of the what's in it for me attitude. Choose to create "how we can all win" solutions.

Time spent nurturing, loving, learning, and laughing with others is indeed – quality time.

Thought to ponder – Engaging with others builds to connect - like souls growing, loving, and laughing together.

Because Young Adults Have Hearts 2!

It is good to help people without expecting something in return.

Thought to ponder – What can you do to build rewarding connections with others? c

SNIPPTIP #6

There is a *passion* side and a directorial side involved with most things that deal with people.

Thought to ponder – It is good for me to understand and embrace the differences in both, so I can do well to help them.

SNIPPTIP #7

View leadership as more than processes, procedures, and order.

Thought to ponder –My leadership style is based on consideration and care for others.

SNIPPTIP #8

Connect yourself to whatever your heart calls you to be a part of, especially things bringing people together.

Thought to ponder – When people are involved, hearts must be considered.

Business is the universal language.

Thought to ponder – What do I want my future to look like? Now, may be the best time to do some purposeful due diligence.

If improving our lives is the reason we are on earth, could helping others help seal one's place in heaven?

Thought to ponder – What are ways I grow by helping someone else?

Truth and ethical values must be the basis of whatever I choose to be a part of.

Thought to ponder – What are a few heart-inspired standards that guide me?

SNIPPTIP #12
Mindfulness of others is contagious.

Thought to ponder – Do my emotional energies have the wherewithal to spread quickly?

SNIPPTIP #13
Change requires action for moving forward.

Thought to ponder – Do I welcome changes, viewing them as a catalyst for my growth?

SNIPPTIP #14
What drives my passion grows from my heart.

Thought to ponder – Why would I not want to share what warms my heart with others?

Being responsive to others shows a high level of care.

Thought to ponder – A smile, an encouraging word, a pat on the back; so many ways to care for the hearts of others.

Thoughtfulness consists of little gestures of care that take root, multiply and spread.

Thought to ponder – Now, how do I react to indifference, what about thoughtfulness – how do these two words influence my heart when dealing with others?

Awareness is not a rare find; it is up to me to make it an intentional act.

Thought to ponder – Paying attention to the nuisances affecting people shows concern.

SNIPPTIP #18

Humility tops the list as a great success builder, as it activates productive synergy among people.

Thought to ponder – Being fake takes much work. Does my genuine care for others flow easily from within?

SNIPPTIP #19

The journey to success is a steady movement toward the goal. Success is not a destination, but the many accomplished steps along the way. Success, then, as well as failure is not accidental.

Thought to ponder – Success looks different to everyone. What does success look like to me?

SNIPPTIP #20

Whatever I pursue, I realize it is not only what it produces in my life, but what it may bring into other people's lives as well.

Thought to ponder – What are some ways to be more thoughtful to others?

I realize what I do, what I say, and how I behave is watched.

Thought to ponder – I desire to do what is right.

A setback is a lesson to learn. If one way does not work, try another. Uncovering the lesson in the good, the bad, and the ugly experiences often become great blessings.

Thought to ponder – What learning style helps me to continue to better my best?

Staying focus requires daily attention.

Thought to ponder – Where does my daydreaming take me to better my heart?

SNIPPTIP #24

Intuition is a self-activating power requiring close attention.

Thought to ponder – What can I do to nurture my intuition to help others?

SNIPPTIP #25

Acceptance of others is a great way to grow my heart.

Thought to ponder – Now, what about tolerance. Do I practice acceptance as better than tolerance?

SNIPPTIP #26

There are many offerings to help me grow.

Thought to ponder – How do I assure what is offered is beneficial and healthy for my growth?

Never enough! Every day is a day to answer the question, "what will keep me moving forward".

Thought to ponder – Now, we all learn by asking the hard questions. I will not just accept, but learn the answer to "why"?

Find ways to stir my creative energies.

Thought to ponder – Doing what I love soars my enthusiastic passion to result in something great.

Have I taken the time to create my personal goals?

Thought to ponder – I realize my goals must be flexible so they may be adjusted as needed.

Short-term goals are necessary as a survival mode. Long-term goals create growth. As a Leader growing, I must break away from the survival approach, and anticipate contingencies to thrive.

Thought to ponder – What are some ways to re-vamp, re-new and revitalize my strengths every day?

Knowing my purpose feeds my heart good.

Thought to ponder – It is good to know where I am headed. It is good knowing my "Why".

I understand the importance of keeping my vision in plain sight.

Thought to ponder – Are my daily activities on point for reaching my goals?

Life demands a constant focus on both the positive and negative happenings.

Thought to ponder –Yes, indeed – I'll savor the good while pulling the good from the (seemingly) bad events of life.

Quietness is a splendid way to stir creative thinking.

Thought to ponder – It is great to listen from within.

I consider myself part of the team, as there is no I in the word team.

Thought to ponder – Now, do my actions, as well as my words, match my perceived role?

It's important to seek ways to implement positive stimuli to keep my heart on fire.

Thought to ponder – What are some things I can do to keep my heart blossoming and moving?

I must remember not to become so focused on my goal that I forget about others.

Thought to ponder – How will I make the time to care about someone else?

Start with the end in mind.

Thought to ponder – Can knowing the results I desire help me create steps to get there?

"What's in it for me?"

Thought to ponder – When asking yourself this question, make sure the answer provides great value, not just for yourself, but for others as well.

As a leader, I value being known as a resource.

Thought to ponder – How can your growth to help empower others?

I love to share my energies with those I interact with.

Thought to ponder – Have I taken the time to filter my effect on others?

SNIPPTIP #42

I'll remember to speak, not so much to impress, but to inspire.

Thought to ponder – What I say I will do is not as important as what I do. Is this true or false? Why?

SNIPPTIP #43

Establish patterns for success.
Thought to ponder – What are some ways I can outperform my best efforts?

SNIPPTIP #44

Clean up your mess! Is this another way of saying, be true and accountable to yourself?

Thought to ponder – Because self-talk comes from a trusted source, how does it aid my growth?

SNIPPTIP #45

Work hard to keep things simple. Mistakes often result when things are overly complicated.

Thought to ponder – How do I, first, correct the mistake. Second, how will I use it as a lesson of growth?

As a grow Leader, I am choosing to embrace challenges, choices, and change.

Thought to ponder – Challenges, choices, and change are life's growth patterns. How will they help to better me?

Believe my caring spirit makes whatever I touch special

Thought to ponder – Treasure own success as a roadmap to help others reach success.

Indifference toward others is not only cold, but un-productive.

Thought to ponder – Do I realize how my indifference affect others and how easily it can spread?

SNIPPTIP #49
If I'm the only one talking – something is not working.

Thought to ponder – How do I encourage trust, so others voice their opinions?

SNIPPTIP #50
Whatever I choose to be a part of, I hope to be a part helping it to be the best it can be.

Thought to ponder – Perfection is not the goal, excellence is desired, are they one and the same?

SNIPPTIP #51

As a Leaders growing, my words can build up walls or tear them down.

Thought to ponder – I choose to grow authentic connections with people.

Opportunities involve risk. I will investigate and make a decision and keep it moving.

Thought to ponder – Now, How do I measure the pros and cons to arrive at the best decision?

As a Leader growing, it is my desire to be a purposeful mentor to others.

Thought to ponder – My intent is to bring value to others.

I'll nurture the relations I have with others.

Thought to ponder – How do I grow this connectedness created?

SNIPPTIP #55
Believe that great leadership ability lies within everyone.

Thought to ponder – As I grow my leadership ability, I'll help others embrace this trait in themselves.

SNIPPTIP #56
What is this unique experience often called friends?

Thought to ponder – Is Leadership simply creating mutually beneficial friendships?

SNIPPTIP #57
A major way to grow hearts is with open, honest, and purposeful communication.

Thought to ponder – What are some non-verbal ways to convey care for others?

Know that self-motivation is not a luxury. It is essential for growth. Stay in proactive mode; never wait on external forces to trigger your leadership action.

Thought to ponder – What keeps you moving forward?

1. passion
2. values

Thought to ponder – How can the above two words help you care for the hearts of others?

Whatever you do, know that real progress stems from beneficial relationships.

Thought to ponder – Think of creative ways to develop and nurture the relationships in your life.

SNIPPTIP #61

To warm a heart, let them see your heart.

Thought to ponder – What is the true value of a rewarding relationship, because helping someone is not always a one-way street.

SNIPPTIP #62

Be proud as no one will do it like you.

Thought to ponder – How do you create the knowledge, tie, energy and hart needed to grow your "it"?

SNIPPTIP #63

Strive to help others.

Thought to ponder – I realize this "Help" may often be simply listening – is this a higher level of care?

SNIPPTIP #64

I am a Leader growing – striving to boost the "whole team".

Thought to ponder – What are some ways to encourage each person's support of the whole?

It is a good feeling when my energies help to create something amazing.

Thought to ponder – What is something someone can boast about me? Not to brag, but understanding what I share and how to improve.

Care for others defines my leadership personality.

Thought to ponder – Fairness and correctness are part of helping people that keeps my heart authentic.

Kaizen - far-reaching results through constant and continuous improvement.

Thought to ponder – What do I need to do to grow every day?

Appreciate the world of business shows no favorites.

Thought to ponder – It all starts within. Do you believe you have the wherewithal for success?

Personal success creates success for others.

Thought to ponder – As a Leader growing you embrace the power of care, as it results spreads.

Respect, a little word with gargantuan impact.

Thought to ponder – What makes the effects of respect so important?

Connecting people and information sets the tone for **win-win** situations.

Thought to ponder – Should caring for people be at the top of a Leader's agenda?

As a hearts-fed and hearts-led young leader, strive to be someone others go to for help.

Thought to ponder – Because growth is constant, how do you better your best?

Is your passion something that warms your heart, and does it help others?

Thought to ponder – How do you know if your passion, your "It" is giving people what you intend it to?

SNIPPTIP #74

Aim for winning connections with everyone.

Thought to ponder – How do you grow you?

SNIPPTIP #75

Growth of anything takes commitment, time, and energy.

Thought to ponder – How do you create quality time just for you?

SNIPPTIP #76

To grow your heart, feed it Life's good.

Thought to ponder – How do you share Life's good with others?

SNIPPTIP #77

Handle Life's good and her (seemingly) bad with the warmth of your heart.

Thought to ponder – Now, are you the example, inviting others to follow your lead?

It is not always right or wrong.

Thought to ponder – Sometimes; it is just How can we all get along?

Listen to your thoughts, trust that inner knowing to move forward with purpose.

Thought to ponder – How does your instinct pave way for strong, warm, and heart-involved relationships.

Make it a daily requirement to give smiles away. How hard it is to be angry, upset, jealous, or sad if you are smiling.

Thought to ponder – When you catch a frown, how do you turn it around?

The awesome power of words.

Thought to ponder – How might the following words influence who you are?

Reserved	Giving
Friendly	Resourceful
Ethical	Risk-taker
Creative	Advocate
Encourager	Focused
Purposeful	Sensitive
Passionate	Intuitive

Continue adding words that can become motivating practices strengthening your heart and the hearts of others.

Discernment is major in understanding others.

Thought to ponder – How do you embrace the different gifts of others?

Claim I Can; it becomes "I Will".

Thought to ponder – How do you embrace the leadership skill, "I Will", to bring out the best in you?

Growing your heart is a lifetime commitment; it is a lifestyle.

Thought to ponder – Does the status of your heart reflect who you are and what you are about?

Be sure your passion feeds your heart good.

Thought to ponder – Heart-focused initiatives feeds hearts good. Heart-focused initiatives grows people.

SNIPPTIP #86

The best learning is teaching as it keeps knowledge in motion.

Thought to ponder – How do you keep knowledge moving for yourself and then, to actively pass on to others?

SNIPPTIP #87

Hello – yes, there are rules.

Thought to ponder – What is the major "golden" rule of your heart as a Leader growing?

SNIPPTIP #88

Young heart – you are an authentic leader with the ability and confidence in yourself to help others by way of your heart.

Thought to ponder – You possess what is required to be a powerful and empowering leader – your perfect gift of a Heart!

So, here you have them...

- 88 intentional ways to feed hearts good today, tomorrow, and always.

- 88 sparkling ways to keep knowledge in motion, your own and others.

- 88 mini lessons creating love and spreading it.

- 88 daily affirmations for growth.

- **88 reminders of the awesomeness of love in the heart growing, spreading and touching other hearts!**

***

MORE SNIPPTIPS...

- Faith in yourself and the good in people feeds hearts good.

- Focus on purposeful, productive, and harmonious living.

- Seek ways to expand personal and professional networks.

- Work hard to give more than you receive.

- Practice the art of leaving heart pieces everywhere.

- Work continuously to better your inner spirit.

- Love what you do and how it helps others.

- Believe Today is the best of times.

- Strive for excellence by bettering your best.

- Embrace challenges as lessons to learn or classes to re-take.

- Stand ready to "fight"; a good life is not a given but earned.

- Keep your heart primed, and talents ready to help people.

- Let go of life's disposals, cherish the keepsakes that grow hearts.

- Care for the hearts of others by creating, growing, and sharing.

- Love quiet times with self.

- Use your strengths and weaknesses for growth.

- Adapt to fit the need of the situation.

Because Young Adults Have Hearts 2!

- Start with people where they are.

- Own your leadership strengths.

- Act as one among people.

- Focus on moving forward.

***

Heart Pulse Strengths

Self-knowing *by way of* self-exploration *nurtures* the heart…

Assign each strength a pulse 1 to 3
1 = weak   2 = good   3 = strong

__Proactive, more than reactive about life

__A winner even if things do not go as planned

__Maintain a positive attitude about life

__Driven by a WIN (what's important now) approach

__Seek new and or better ways of doing the same thing

__Go the extra step to assist people

__Self-motivated to excel

__Honest enthusiasm for helping others

__Continual learner always striving to better best self

__Filled with a "do it NOW" attitude

__Genuinely interested in serving people

__Treasure reputation for fairness and sincerity

__Believe in hard work

__Faith in self to handle almost any situation

__Focus more on growing strengths than overcoming faults

__Proud to be known as a viable resource

__Forward-thinker – removed the BOX

__Treat people the way EXPECT to be treated

__View self as responsive and resourceful

__Proud of own principled standards

__Re-invent, re-package, and revamp self when needed

__Proud to consider self a growing Leader

__Practice "pay-it-forward" tactics with people

__Continuously grow "If I Believe I Can, I will" mindset

__A proponent of prepare, prepare, prepare…

__Easily adapt to the "needed" position for any situation

__Utilize the power of questions

__Embrace the power in purposeful awareness

__Listen carefully to heart when dealing with people

__Embrace the power of routine

__Make the best decision; then move forward on purpose

__Always keep commitments to self

__Embrace the social (heart) side of business endeavors

__Always seeking ways to connect with people

__Stimulate self with purposeful and loving self-talk

__Embrace powers of short-term as well as long-term goals

__Pay the price of power - to empower others

__Embrace the lesson from all experiences

__Know what to fight for and what to compromise on

__Not fear failing; it is a lesson gleaned moving to success

__Goes through a problem to resolve it – not around it

RESULTS - no failures here, just heart-loving Leaders growing…

| 52-98 | **Caring leadership behaviors** |

| 99+ | **Hearts-fed to hearts-led Leader** |

***

Section 4

Special Pieces...

- We are Leaders...

- Ten Directives for Loving You!

- Keeping Your Heart in Motion...

- 10 Must-haves for a Gracious...

- Outstanding Leaders <u>Stand</u>...

- Hearts-fed to Hearts-led <u>LEADERS</u>...

***

As a growing Leader, I Am...

- extremely motivated to excel

- embracing the powers of my heart

- valuing blessings by being a blessing

- using my energies for rewarding connections

- an ordinary person with an extraordinary need to share

- helping others find opportunities in their good and (seemingly) bad happenings

- embracing the life-changing powers of faith

- aware my enthusiasm and my indifference are highly contagious

- cultivating a proactive spirit, not counting on hope, and wishing

- seeking facts versus settling for the opinions of others

- loving, learning, and laughing every day

- leaving my mark, not for fame or glory, but for making someone's life better

***

Ten Directives for Loving YOU!

#1   Perfect Imperfections
Accept your humanness; perfection is so boring.
Bettering your best – now, that is exhilarating.

#2   Positive View
It is not what happens to us, but how we react that determines the shape and validity of the lesson. Whether it is your day to soar, or be still, **discover** the lesson in all your experiences.

#3   Internal Power
Believe in yourself. Know who you are. Outside forces may ignite the passion, but internal desire will keep it blazing for the long haul. **Nurture** you constant states of changes that lead to growth.

#4   Acceptance Love

Life creates many opportunities to "mess up". How long will you beat yourself for past mistakes? How many "if only" sighs will you utter? Sincerely apologize to those you hurt, especially yourself. **Move** on, you are stronger from the experience.

#5 Best Competition

Why compete with someone else? Be your greatest competitor by **improving** your best. Decide what is best for you, not because of anyone or anything else, but you.

#6 Purposeful Moves

Focus on the task and keep moving. Yes, life will throw you off balance, but keep forging on. Do not stop – do not be deterred but **move** forward on purpose.

#7 Falling Up

How many times do we watch toddlers stumble and fall? We encourage them "try it again". We need to adopt this attitude for ourselves. Know this - **getting up**, dusting off, and forging ahead is the shape of one's worthiness.

#8   Reinforce Self

It is more than okay to pat yourself on the back; it is a necessity. **Be** comfortable with your greatness. It is not ego-tripping to appreciate who you are and what you are about. Appreciate reinforcement from others but cherish own feelings of self.

#9   Follow the Leader

Who defines a follower or a Leader? Do not shortchange your leadership abilities. Allow your charismatic style to activate exceptional leadership influences with people. **Follow** today; **lead** tomorrow, it's your call, so set the pace that is right for you.

#10   Radiant YOU!

Loving yourself is not a destination; it is a lifelong journey. You are not the person you were yesterday, nor the person you will be tomorrow. You are evolving, bettering your best every day. Have an exciting trip being you as you learn, laugh, love, and grow, discovering your brilliance.

Because loving you <u>Better</u> makes it easier to love others <u>More</u>!

***

Keeping YOUR Heart in Motion...

- Decide to grow from a position of love. Make it fun to seek out ways to be a better you.

- Always be honest, especially with yourself.

- Helping someone is a sure way to help yourself, so scatter positive influences everywhere you go.

- Embrace the joy that resides within while fostering outer happiness.

- Let go of that spirit of entitlement - grow your thankfulness.

- Pay more attention to where you are headed than what you left behind.

- Be grateful Today, tomorrow is not promised.

- Always check your own mirror first by being accountable to yourself.

- Pay it forward by helping someone.

- Questions empower – question yourself and grow.

- Be grateful for all life's lessons as many become blessings.

- Choose to laugh often. Laugh at yourself and laugh with others. Have fun and do not take yourself too seriously.

Now, the operative word is Love. Because Love makes the world go around, keep loving in motion. Grow the love that was gifted to you at birth, allowing it to blossom and spread to those you touch.

***

10 Must-haves for a Gracious, Growing and Giving Heart!

1. **Care for outside influences but cherish and pay keen attention to that inner knowing more**.

    a. There are times to tune out the outside and tune more into the wisdom from within.

    b. Do not try to stop the negative thoughts (they will pop up); – instead, discover the source of the negative thought and find ways to use it to grow.

    c. Listen to what you say to yourself. Discard what is not kind, loving and encouraging. Replace with loving and stimulating self-talk. Realize, it is more important what you say to yourself than what you say to others.

    d. Practice mindfulness. Paying attention to what is happening around you produces thoughts and actions that will teach and guide you.

    e. Quiet yourself. Be still. Think about zilch.

2.   Trust your inner knowing. Develop and pay attention to it always. Treat it as the treasure it is by feeding your senses with meaningful conversations with yourself.

3.   Feed your heart well with whatever makes your spirit soar.   Nurture your passion - Enjoy your passion – Share your passion.

4.   Be your own best friend … Honor all commitments to self - be honest with self - uphold ethical standards - realize it's all about "Your" attitude.

5.   Learn from your mistakes. Grow stronger from your mistakes allowing them to become lessons learned.

6.   Don't fight so hard to be liked by others, fight hard to like yourself. Feel good about the way others see you, but know it is more important you see yourself as the kind, loving and helpful person you are. Always know, you are your own hero!

7. **Be prideful of who you are and what you care about**. It is ok, in fact, it is mandatory to pat yourself on the back.

8. **Treasure the unseen forces of life**. What we do not see often provides more power than the visible.

9. **Always look for the best in others**. The Almighty God makes NO mistakes. He created you and me – there is good in everyone.

10. **Unlock the door to your heart**. The specialness of your heart is bigger than you are, so giving of your heart only makes it stronger.

***

Outstanding Leaders <u>Stand-out</u> ...

A possibility Phenomenon...

Leaders that stand-out *believe* all Life's lessons have within it the wherewithal to become great life blessings. They approach the challenges of Life as opportunities and possibilities.

Embrace being a lifelong Learner!

Leaders that stand-out *realize* the learning never ends, it's a lifelong experience. These Leaders use whatever means necessary to keep themselves informed, capable, and motivated to always better their best.

Realize great results start with Anticipation!

"If you can see it, you can achieve it" is a popular saying. Leaders that stand-out *embrace* the importance of keeping goals in plain sight to be sure they are on the success path.

Grow by aligning strengths with others!

Leaders that stand-out *leverage* their knowing with others. They take pride in collaborating with others to create tremendous value realizing the best win always involves more than one winner.

Keep a constant watch on their hearts.

Leaders that stand-out pay attention to the things and inklings of their heart. They *answer* on the regular, **"What is the landscape of my heart?** Is IT idle, cold, and shrinking, or Is IT active, flourishing, and giving?"

Leaders that stand-out keep their hearts in learning, laughing, loving, and growing mode. They do what it takes to keep it there.

***

Hearts-fed to hearts-led
<u>LEADERS</u>...

<u>L</u>isten to the pull within; share your heart.

<u>E</u>nergize someone – help with what's important now.

<u>A</u>ctively help someone plant success seed.

<u>D</u>o what's in your power to support someone's dream.

<u>E</u>ducate others by your actions.

<u>R</u>einforce relationships.

<u>S</u>tep up and share You.

***

Section 5

End Pieces

Three special designs of:

Corporate **<u>SNIPPETS</u>** -

The Company of ...

- The word *because* is used numerous times as channels to learning, laughing, loving, and growing.

- The concepts used for *loving hearts* are showcased in different styles to highlight and affirm their importance.

- The entirety of this publication points to one thing - *the importance of caring for hearts!*

Not the end ...
A beginning

The Company of
•••

***

Corporate <u>SNIPPETS</u>–
The Company of ...

Dear Reader:

The original intent of this book was to serve as a business toolbox, a lifestyle manual, a spiritual digest, basically a *how-to* help people by way of the heart.

The initial review by the Board – "It is a great book, it shows you put a lot of thought and effort and your heart and soul into it, and people will love it – <u>BUT</u>"!

Followed Board's advice to not make it a one fit all read.   So, thanks to the Board, my greatest supporter, my beautiful daughter LaLa.

Because Young Adults Have Hearts 2!

Corporate **SNIPPETS** – The Company of ...

Because **Women** Have *Hearts* 2!

Because **Young Adults** Have *Hearts* 2!

Because **Ministries** Have *Hearts* 2!

Because **Leaders** Have *Hearts* 2!

***

Writer/Influencer/Leader, TR Ford

TR says a blank piece of paper is not safe around her, as it soon becomes full of ideas and thoughts for feeding hearts good, her own, and others.

TR is building a legacy of feeding hearts good and desires this publication to enlighten, entertain, and stimulate people's hearts.

TR invites young adults to know that leadership is within their reach. It is not about age, it's not about a title, it is not about gender, and certainly, it's not about one's position.

Simply, great leadership is loving people enough to share your heart to help them grow.

This is your power, young hearts.

She encourages Young Adults *to step - step boldly, step proudly* and *step purposefully* to lend a hand and help someone.

You have a caring heart – you are a Leader.

The Company of ...

Feed your heart good, feed it often and share the feed to enjoy love always.

TR

P.S. Whether this material is applicable in your life today or if it is tomorrow; please know that whatever warms, grows, excites, and loves your heart is relevant in your life now.

Allow this material to strengthen your heart to help you care for the hearts of others.

SUNSHINE 4 HEARTS

where love lives, blossoms, and spreads.

404-491-2933

Sunshine4Hearts!

Corporate **SNIPPETS** because Young Adults
Have *Hearts* 2!

***

www.ingramcontent.com/pod-product-compliance
Lightning Source LLC
Chambersburg PA
CBHW070343220526
45467CB00001B/235